I Had to Laugh tc

MW00395513

How Humor Saved My Life!

A Survivor's Story

Written by Maureen Joy

Edited by Julie A. Roberts

(Editor (Formerly Chief Editor) at Conscious Community Magazine

2013-Present)

Foreword

Humor helps us cope in crisis by momentarily altering our state. You can't feel positive, hopeful, and/or enthusiastic in the middle of a traumatic loss; it shouldn't even be expected! But in working through the grief, you need to balance the "work" with a "warm fuzzy!" If someone gives you a hot cup of cocoa or an aromatic, tasty, warm drink when you are cold and shaking, it is soothing and makes you feel good, EVEN IF YOU ARE MISERABLE! For a moment, you can focus on the warmth flowing inside of you... for a moment, you feel OK. That's what humor is; it is the hot cocoa with marshmallows when you're shivering and your body is wracked. It is a moment of a soothing "warm fuzzy" for your spirit.

H – Hopeful

U – Universal/Uplifting

M – Mood-Altering

O – Open-Hearted

R – Release

My story of rediscovery and deeper understanding of the healing powers of humor is a tragic one. My only sister, Jill, whom as an adult I was inseparable from, was brutally murdered on December 16, 1991. That year was the most horrific year of my life! I still recall the day I heard the "news" ...it came from over the phone in a detached, cold, and brutal call from my distant father. I was at my grandmother's house visiting, as I often did. The news was on television, but I wasn't paying much attention to it as usual. Gram and I were talking about "life" stuff, which was of much greater interest to me than the "crap" they called "news!" Little did I know that my apathy would turn to disdain and outrage for the blatant form of desensitization that contributed to the unbearable agony of what was to become my life after Jill's murder.

DEDICATION

This book is dedicated to my mom, Fran, and my beloved sister Jill, who helped me become who I am today. Our relationship was the closest bond of unconditional love that I experienced in my life. My sister taught me how to be grounded, to appreciate and respect nature, experience the wonderment of the constellations, and always encouraged me to reach for the stars. My mother taught me kindness, compassion and empathy. Her vivacious, free-spirited nature was infectious, and attracted people everywhere we went. She had the inner strength and fortitude of a warrior, and taught me to be independent. Two strong women I carry with me in my heart, and along my *Healing Journey*, to guide and support me along my path, and to always "Pay It Forward!"

GRATITUDE

I give gratitude to all of the loving people who have come into my life, then, now, and in the future; who support and encourage me to share my impetus in the world to touch people's hearts, through my words and music, with a message encouraging Survivors to embrace their own *Healing Journey*.

Contents

Chapter One: The Beginning of the End

My name is Maureen Joy. My story of how laughter and humor saved my life started with a tragedy. My only baby sister, Jill, was killed when we were in our 20s! To say I was unable to function was an understatement! I was beyond devastated… I was destroyed!

I was always someone who had a passion for personal growth. So naturally, I would seek answers and solutions as to how I was to live as a Homicide Survivor. I was always able to reach out and ask for help, and this was absolutely necessary to my survival! I was living in a suburb where there was an outreach center, and when the director heard of my plight, she volunteered to take me on as a client. She was a godsend, as were so many others who helped me put some semblance of a life back together after I lost my sister… my best friend.

I was so lost… I walked around wiping back tears for years. The first two years I was basically homebound and bedridden. I found it nearly impossible to re-enter the world; I went into hiding for a long time! My days consisted of reading books to help me heal, seeing my counselor, going to support groups, journaling, and of course crying… a lot! For years, I could barely put one foot in front of the other. I found very little enjoyment in things I loved when Jill was alive. We were bonded on a deeper level than many siblings were. She was the grounded one… I was the artist, the drama queen. I was very sensitive, emotional, and passionate. When Jill was alive, my star shined bright. When she was killed, I felt my shine die out with just barely a spark of life grasping to be remembered.

For a long time, I dragged what felt like a dead body around inside me. I was a mess! I was extremely depressed, angry, confused, and apathetic towards life and God. I struggled with faith for many years. How could a loving God allow this tragedy and many other horrific events in the world? I turned to my music… I purged my pain! I found some sense of solace in singing from my heart and soul, which on my CD, *Healing Journey* often sounds like my gut. My haunting sound at times even sent a chill down my own spine… and I was the one creating the sound!

Mom and I knew how necessary it was to get support, so we attended support groups for Homicide Survivors: Parents Of Murdered Children (POMC), and the international grief support group The Compassionate Friends. We were both desperate to find a reason to want to live! At this point, neither of us did.

We were incapable of resuming our lives before Jill was killed. Every day was a challenge to just get out of bed!

I remember being at a conference where 5000 people and families who had lost loved ones gathered at the Hyatt Hotel in downtown Chicago in the early 2000's. There were individual groups for us to attend: parents, siblings, spouses. I will never forget the response to my sharing from my group leader. He said to me with such kindness in his eyes, "It must take an enormous effort on your part, Maureen, to just put one foot in front of the other."

Yes! He got it! I remember how I felt heard, seen, and validated by this man's compassion towards me. It was then I realized people who are grieving (and who have gone through trauma) must be validated. Their feelings must be heard, recognized, and honored in order for them to heal.

Even with all of my knowledge and information, I still struggled with intense grief. I had to find a purpose through my pain in order to choose to live and reconnect in the world again. In order to survive, I had to find my reason *why*. At the time, I had a very surly disposition and quickly humored everyone I came across. I actually found nothing to laugh about… ironically, this is when you need humor most! Even in my darkest, moodiest space, I could laugh when I watched a comedy, or heard or read something I got a kick out of. It felt foreign in the beginning… almost as if I felt it was a betrayal to my grief. That thought and belief was soon replaced by healthier ones - humor allows grief to be palatable!

So, I immersed myself in everything relating to humor and healing that I could get my hands on. I developed a program using humor to enhance the workplace, and increase company net worth by creating a convivial environment where employees could thrive, and even enjoy their workday. I did this for years, and eventually, I formed a promotion company where I represented musicians, artists, speakers, authors, and a theatre company.

I couldn't sustain doing a lot, but I was able to create and go out into the world in small increments. After a few hours, I found myself needing to retreat back into my now more reclusive lifestyle. This is totally opposite of the girl I was when my sister was alive.

Then, I was on fire! I had Rock-It Promotions, I modeled and acted, I was a ring girl for kickboxing, and I had a character role on *Windy City Wrestling,* playing a fabulous blonde alter ego! I was very private and I always loved to costume. I danced since I was three years old and I was very comfortable with the sequins and fringe. Yes, I had a few years under my belt at this point. But when Jill was killed it was as if I died that day along with her.

Hysterical, though heavily sedated at her funeral, I could barely stand to read the poem I wrote for her service, "I Will Remember You." I couldn't have made it without the love and support from my boyfriend at the time. Michael was my angel. He took care of me at my worst, and there was worse!

Three months prior to Jill's murder, I fell from his six-foot-two-inch shoulders at a concert and onto cement, face first. It was a gruesome, bloody mess! I had my face in bandages for months, which he lovingly cleaned and changed daily. I will never forget this. Our relationship, though extremely loving, couldn't withstand the blow of my sister's murder. He couldn't stay long-term with the woman I turned into… a mess! He met me as a confident, self-assured, outgoing, fun-loving partner. I became a reclusive, dark, morbid, surly, depressed mess who woke up screaming at night. He left. That became another loss to deal with. My thoughts: Man plans, God laughs! Even in extreme sadness, I could find humor in my own outlandish thoughts and antics.

Humor saved my life! Music soothed my soul! Sharing my *Healing Journey* with the world serves my purpose!

Chapter Two: The Case of the Runaway Underpants

It was our first and only Homicide Survivors meeting… Mom was fidgeting and I was uncomfortable, but we were there with other grieving family members. We were desperate to find people who could relate and validate our pain without needing the "frothy" details! That is what really angered us most of all. It was through Mom's fidgeting that I discovered how healing laughter is for the body and spirit… Mom too. As we sat quietly, waiting for our turn to burst open, I noticed my mother nervously pulling at something at the bottom of her pant leg. Her refreshingly open desire to examine the material she now produced as the "thing" attached to the dangling "string" left me both aghast and relieved to release the now uncontrollable laughter that we had fought so hard to repress - she was holding a huge pair of underpants above the table in plain sight! We couldn't wait to get out of that meeting so we could fully allow ourselves a much needed, pent up release of laughter. We laughed at both the incident; it couldn't have been more inappropriate if we had planned it that way, and how my sister, Jill, the reason we were at a Homicide Survivors meeting, would have disowned both of us for our embarrassing antics! Jill owned the book *Miss Manners' Guide to Excruciatingly Correct Behavior*… this was a definite faux-pas!

We loved how good it felt to laugh! That night in the car, we decided we would fill our lives with as much humor as we could gather. Mom and I were always clowning around in our own eccentric way. It makes perfect sense that I would seek refuge in humor and eventually incorporate a healing program encompassing the cathartic release humor provides. In humor, I could escape. There was hope, even if it was only for a moment, that tomorrow could be OK. Eventually, in time, my heart palpitations would cease. It took many years, and a lot of hard grief work, not to mention all the hours spent balancing the "icky" stuff with my new humor library, but the heart palpitations finally ceased. I'm still very sad, and I will always be miserable at certain anniversary dates, holidays, birthdays, and other unexpected triggers. But I'm now reinventing my life and incorporating everything and anything I can get my hands on that is related to how humor heals the mind, body, and spirit.

Although I wasn't sure how, I knew I wanted to share my healing process with the world. The worst part of it was reliving the horror as I wrote. However, two days after the seventh anniversary of Jill's murder, I'm pleased that I sat down and just flowed with the process. It was always important to have a life purpose, but now it has become essential! I choose to be enlightened, empathic, and an educator, while I continue to reconstruct my life.

I hope the wrought-out emotions of the experiences I went through would be conviction to readers that there was nothing for me or mom to laugh about… humor didn't come easy, and most of mine was my flippant disposition matter-of-factly stating whatever came to mind. Other people laughed at the way I "said" things. Even when I was acting out, my facetious attitude caused unyielding uproars on my account. Even when I was miserable, I could get a spark of delight from myself and my own antics – even if only for a moment, at times.

I noticed that at these moments, I was a little more (dare I say) hopeful. I wasn't happy, and I didn't want anyone expecting that from me. The idea was astronomical! But, if I chose to let in a little "warm fuzzy," I found I really loved the release humor gave me; I ranked it right up there with sex for things to live for! I realized at this moment that I must look into this humor and healing idea I had. I was always interested in learning new ways to improve my life. Now it wasn't merely a curiosity, it was a necessity! I always found great comfort in reading self-help manuscripts, but now I was on a mission - a mission to save my life!

I knew I couldn't survive the way I was: I barely slept, and if I did sleep, it was interrupted. I was barely eating and having extreme stress on my heart. If I didn't find answers sooner rather than later... I decided to immerse myself in everything I could get my hands on relating to how humor heals. I read about different people, like Norman Cousins, a man who unknowingly fell upon how laughing helped him to lessen his intense pain of a diagnosis he suffered with when the pain meds wore off. He was watching one of his favorite comedies, *The Three Stooges*, when he realized that he wasn't feeling the intense discomfort he usually had to bear. He, like myself decades later, stumbled upon the healing power of humor. He was the catalyst of many like myself who jumped on this bandwagon and rode it all the way to relief!

Another preceding Humor Advocate was Patch Adams. He was an intern in a hospital and realized he needed to lighten the intense pain and suffering of cancer patients, especially children in the hospital he worked at. He brought out all of his funny antics, props, and a great attitude when working with these very ill patients. He saw that they were laughing and there was a ray of joy in their eyes when he visited them. Patch Adams brought humor into a clinical, previously sterile, environment where it was life-altering for many! I was so moved by him when I read his story that I created a program titled "Humor, Health and Healing," which I intended to share as a speaker with other Survivors.

My first endeavor at integrating humor as a healing tool was when I decided to surround myself with *everything* I could find that made me laugh out loud. I found movies, television shows, audiobooks, comedians, and magazine cutouts that I displayed all over my living space.

I found jokes that made me laugh, and put Post-it notes on the mirrors as well as cute props like my "toy" boyfriend. When you pull his string, he says all the right things! It always made me laugh to do this as it was a far cry from what came out of most of the guys' mouths I dated after my relationship with Michael ended. My taste in men was in itself laughable! As another avenue to pursue, I developed an interactive comedy show in Chicago and the suburbs where I spoofed a lingerie and modeling "business." It was like *Seinfeld* meets *The Nanny* in thigh-high boots and other outrageous costumes! I told stories about my exploits with men and jokes. They always yielded uproarious laughter and applause, which I loved!

I couldn't go back to work, but I had to find a way to survive in the world on my own terms. The western society way didn't allow me to heal. I was so livid that people are actually expected to just go back and resume life as it was after a tragic death! How ridiculous! This angered me and I had a difficult time relating with others who expected this of me or anyone else in my shoes. The other thing I did that saved me was I turned off the news, and never picked up a newspaper again. I refuse to read or listen to the negative garbage that they shove down our throats. Yes, I have strong opinions and I adamantly strive to surround myself with positive people, places, and things. I try to eliminate as much negative energy as possible.

Many great Consciousness Thought Leaders do or did the same thing. Somewhere along the line we realized that in order to heal, you need to create a convivial healing environment, which is not easy living in this world. But in my case, it was life or death! I could easily slip if I didn't watch my footing. I was so raw inside and so beaten down that a diet of negativity would destroy me. I wouldn't be here today if I didn't find and incorporate my daily humor regimen along with all of the other healing tools I've garnered. Humor made the necessary grief work palatable!

I needed intense grief therapy, attended numerous seminars on grief and healing, went to many support groups, conferences, as well as studying integrative healing modalities to survive and eventually thrive in the world. I look for humor in things that come my way, and although at times this can be quite challenging, I remind myself that I can choose how I want to show up in the world. When you survive a trauma, *Victimization* is a *Fact*, but to stay a *Victim* is a *Choice*. I'm NOT a *Victim*!

I was traumatized, I suffered cumulus losses, more than many, and shit happened! That said, I choose to be a victor and to continue to incorporate healing tools such as humor in order to live my best life possible.

Chapter Three: Humor and Misery, the Odd Couple That Lives With Me

For years, I've tried to put my *Healing Journey* into words, but each attempt seemed to bring up unbearable pain, which I chose to avoid. Every attempt left me drained and useless for weeks on end! I still recall my most triumphant endeavor to raise the awareness of the general public regarding the issues we Survivors of murdered loved ones' experience. This was at the Democratic Convention at one of the speaking platforms in my home town of Chicago. I spoke to a group of prospective candidates to be enlightened. If I could only reach one person, then my efforts will not have gone unnoticed. If even one person could feel the pain and trauma of what it felt like to have to re-live the horror of your sister's murder on the big screen, totally and fervently against your will…then I will have done my job!

Unfortunately, we live in a society that encourages the media to sensationalize & capitalize on real tragedies. Their blatant apathy towards how their misconstrued "story" is portrayed rubs salt in the wounds of the survivors left behind. More often than not, the "story" they portray on the big screen lacks the truth; a deeper truth that only those who lived it would know. Speaking for many survivors who have lost family members in a violent manner, the last thing we want or need is a media frenzy! It stops the healing process in its tracks! It creates even more pain/angst to have to process!

To have to muster up every ounce of courage to confront the greedy director, begging him not to kick us when we were down… and then be confronted with his cold-hearted refusal to accept any responsibility for capitalizing on our pain! We were treated like a lamb offered up for sacrifice, because the "ritual" gave permission! I refused to bury my head in the sand and decided to show them that when lives are in jeopardy, their free-enterprise jargon loses its validity! Any feeling human being would have been affected by even the slightest pang of guilt. This poor excuse for a human felt no remorse, no responsibility to my mother, who begged him in tears over the phone to hear her. He had no concern at all about the damage and disruption of her only living daughter, who was barely functioning! Could he give a damn about anything aside from their profit margin? I think not!

I decided at *MY* press conference to impede the movie from being made, not to name names regarding the production company, and any publicity. I would reserve my energy to educate and raise awareness amongst those with clout and position strong enough to counter these people in Hollywood; those who jump on our human tragedies and commercialize our pain, when it is against our will and stultifies our grieving process! Talking to the directors and other business tycoons whose only focus and interest was the bottom dollar fell on deaf ears. I would get more response from a corpse than the coldblooded flesh hounds I had to confront!

Letting go of my fight with them wasn't easy, nor did it come without a constant inner struggle to attack the enemy. My anger and hatred for them was only scratching the surface of what I was actually addressing: how the actions of one affects a society. If we all continue to look out only for ourselves, hiding behind a *Constitution* that was never intended to be used as a tool of manipulation in survival of the fittest, we become what we are today: A society that is violent, angry, disconnected, and desensitized to others' feelings.

It does not surprise me that there are young kids who are killing people. There are those who have no value for anyone's life, including their own.

I realized my quest was bigger than confronting coldblooded capitalists… I needed to tell my story and personalize what the pain looks like to effect any change. I needed to work through my own anger at what was happening to me and how intrusive this was, in order to be able to go out into the community and garner the support I needed to make a difference. My next undertaking encompassed the message I relayed in my press conference: "*Enough is Enough!*" Stand up and be accountable for the role you play and the effect your actions have on others! It is time overdue to start treating others how you want to be treated! If you wouldn't like it, then don't do it to anyone else; have compassion for your fellow human being!

I continued to focus on the importance of awareness of the issues we Survivors struggle with on a daily basis, but I chose to cultivate a new approach to the self-serving free enterprising capitalists who insist they are within their constitutional rights to pillage, rape, torture, and even destroy, as long as their medium is the big screen! I obviously still loathe their detached position, but deep down, some part of me wanted to believe they didn't know the magnitude of the trauma they caused in making these movies when we are grieving our loved ones! Often, as in our situation, there is no closure… to have to even *CONCEPTUALIZE* this, made larger than life is *ENRAGING*! There is no validation of our pain; even worse is how there is no real connection to the *DESTRUCTION* they are *EVOKING*! In my mind, if I could confront them in person and articulate the pain, so they would have to place their loved one's faces on my sister's corpse… and feel what I felt: the inability to breathe without medication and tranquilizers to calm the heart palpitations!

To have to read misconstrued stories that were written for the whole world to view, and to feel no safety in a cruel world that devalues people in a quest for monetary gain. It is beyond challenging to have to cope after just losing the most important person in your world… and feeling no one seems to care.

In person, I was an effective and impactful speaker. I was convinced that, given the appropriate arena and the platform to address my adversaries, I could convey the seriousness and damaging effects releasing a movie replete with incorrect portrayed "facts" would cause. Although I didn't expect to reach everyone, I would settle for affecting one person enough to acknowledge their power, and how any misuse wreaks great havoc, causing a universal effect.

I brainstormed for the years in between the press conference and the convention speech… I came up with a compromise that wouldn't restrict the production company's rights, but was a way to include something at the end of the movie that allows us to speak our minds verbatim and unedited. Unfortunately, my idea was ahead of its time, and we were not allotted the opportunity to relay our position, however, the seeds were planted, and people years later were given this ability to have their commentary.

I ended up paving the way for future Survivors to be given the opportunity to have their own personalized commentary.

At the very least, it would eliminate the rage at people who don't know us drawing conclusions from the disjointed reconstruction of events as they saw to incorrectly portray them.

I feel a platform of this kind would give the grief-stricken family members the dignity to segregate themselves from any connection to what they don't support nor believe in. Once I had my position ironed out, my next step was to present it to the Illinois General Assembly in an attempt to propose legislation that provided this platform. I met with attorneys and other congressional leaders who believed in my passion, and offered assistance and support, as well as introductions to the necessary sources. This was no small task, and up until now, always evoked more pain than I could handle. Today, I'm exhausted, but I'm not immobilized as I've been before. I had to put it all away for almost a year. I had to concentrate on making a living and having a life. I feel I'm getting to a point (I pray this becomes my norm) where I can approach where I left off: to address Congress, to continue with my *Humor, Health, and Healing* project, to publish the song I wrote for Jill *("Survivors – Walk with Pain")*, and to find a creative and cathartic way of integrating everything of meaning, to find my destined place and position in the world.

This would also honor Jill's life, instead of only focusing on her death. This was a lot easier said than done. For me, I constantly battle the two forces inside me who equally share a place in my life: Humor, my love to laugh, the joy of feeling my endorphins dance their "happy dance" …and misery that has every right to show up, and at times linger on a regular basis. Living with this dichotomy to many people sounds absurd, but it is the reality of what I was dealt. I still at times choose to rant and rage, and I give myself permission to do so. I've been through more hell than most people I know! I still never forget the little voice inside me that *craves to laugh and smile… no matter what the tragic reality dictates.*

This escape is probably why my father always accused me of living in my own world… I think I agree with him, and thank God that even when I didn't have the technical terminology, instinctively I knew! Misery loves company… but even forced laughter impedes the downward spiral of grief and depression. The brain doesn't know the difference between what is real and what isn't.

When we laugh, we release the positive endorphins that leads to a shift in attitude. This shift permeates our cells and raises our vibration. This allows us to reframe our distress with an open-minded approach using "tools" from our prefrontal cortex in the brain. Laughter can trick the brain and body into believing "I think things are good…or at least ok." It allows us to make better choices that get our needs met.

No matter what you do in life… *Never Stop Laughing!* When there is nothing in life to laugh about- you need humor most!!

Chapter Four: If I Didn't Laugh… I Would Cry

I'm sure it isn't hard to accept the fact that traumatic experiences put a real strain on relationships – especially with the opposite sex. Imagine bringing to the table a fear of intimacy, lack of faith in duration, and general unease when relating to men. Anything that didn't involve coy flirtation, aloof attention, or blatant seduction threw me off my comfort mark! The seductive lure was the wild ride that usually ended with a crash landing. A lot of my love relationships, including my family members (who are supposed to love you unconditionally), have been very painful and heartbreaking. If anyone deserves to be angry, bitter, and resentful, it's me! But instead, I still smile through the tears and search for comedy in relationships – especially watching comedians talk about their problems in an uplifting manner. I can relate to this and fill my life with it; I've decided not to remain a victim, though victimized.

OK, so for a while, it sucks! But there are many reminders all around me that instill a flicker of hope… as long as there is laughter, I think I will be OK… eventually!

It's no wonder my sister Jill didn't like any of my boyfriends…and there were *parades* of them! It isn't that I slept around, but I slept with the guys who I was really attracted to, way before I was convinced that I wanted them in my life. This change of "heart" appeared to look like a "revolving bedroom door." This was my pattern of destruction… until my last real boyfriend, Michael (who even Jill approved of and wanted me to stay with). But things didn't work out that way for Michael and I… we planned-God laughed!

OK, that was an example of my surly humor, that although I verbalize the statement in jest, underneath I'm pretty pissed off about it. Michael was the first guy who I started slow with (I didn't sleep with him on the first night!). I was going to really put in the effort this time to do it right. We got to really know, appreciate, and generally care for each other. I finally chose a guy who wasn't only sexy (always my first requirement), but kind, loving, and willing to open up to and with me.

The first few months we were admired and envied for being the perfect couple; which we were, for a very short while. We looked fabulous together – we really fit. We were actually born on the same day, in the same month. We were both Leos, born in the summer month of August on the 22nd! He was younger (all the guys I dated were)- this never changed. It was regal when we walked into a room together.

We both had long, flowing manes, tall slender bodies that melted together in a passionate explosion! You get the idea… but something even greater matched and completed the picture. He was similar to my sister Jill in many ways. They had the same mannerisms: both were very intelligent, more introverted, and down to earth, quiet and calm, yet loving and sensitive; a refreshing balance to my dramatic, outgoing, passionate personality.

He, like Jill, got a kick out of me! They both told me that I was a "trip," as a quiet smile spread across their faces! I loved them both… but I loved Jill more than I loved anyone (this had to have hurt Michael… I never wanted to hurt him). When Jill was killed, I knew this was the end of the ride for us. No matter how much we loved each other, my grieving was ugly, messy, and pure hell to live with! He did more for Mom and me than all of our family members. But time wasn't on our side, and we were too young and inexperienced (especially in relationships) to have had the necessary tools to work through it together. We would have had to totally reinvent our relationship. We didn't have the strength nor the stamina at this point; drained of all passion we shared, unable to see past the agony of the present situation (not to mention his own personal "stuff"), it would take a miracle to keep us together. Things got rough in every way, we were living together only two or three months when Jill was killed. We were barely out of our "honeymoon" phase, and together for just six months when we had experienced more loss than many couples experience in a lifetime! This wasn't the best formula for a successful relationship. This was only the end; there were many things that led up to our demise.

I fell on my face from Michael's shoulders at a rock concert; my face was a bloody mess, literally! But he devotedly stayed through my ugliest stage. My face was distorted and in bandages (they were barely off at the time Jill was killed). I was too frightened to look in the mirror, fearing what I might see. He lovingly changed my bandages several times a day. I didn't realize the extent of the damage until the day I looked; he always told me that I was as beautiful as I ever was, and I found comfort in his words that I believed were true.

I was hysterical when the mirror reflected otherwise! I couldn't believe such a gorgeous guy would stay with what I now looked like, but he did. This was true love to me!

I was lucky – my face healed almost perfectly. The scar above my lip was barely noticeable and just gave me character. Jill had the same scar from a fall she took as a little girl on her roller skates. We thought our common imperfection was cool!

I also didn't mention the other losses that would precede the final nuclear bomb. Michael's father was a lot like mine, so I didn't like him much. When he took Michael's money out of his bank account without his permission, you could imagine how angry, confused, and embarrassed he felt. My verbal disdain for his father didn't improve the situation. We spent a miserable weekend! It was some holiday that I don't remember in the summer. He sulked and I ranted contemptuously for not standing up to his father, the thief! I wish I had the skills to support him and maintain my position more quietly, or to myself. That was then… and I didn't have these "relationship" skills. A few more mishaps were thrown into the mix of destruction, but it didn't come to a boil until the aftermath of Jill's murder.

I felt damaged for life! If we broke up, I couldn't imagine ever finding someone again, unless he were also a Homicide Survivor or suffered some other great loss! I didn't believe any other guy could relate to me and vice-versa. This was also Michael's suggestion as he walked out the door for good. Fat chance of that happening! My requirements for a date, let alone mate, were definitive, specific, demanding, and outrageous!

Now, I was going to add the necessity of "him" having to be a Survivor of some violent death or tragedy! That was too tall an order even for **GOD**! Even the consideration of such absurdity made me question if my mind was at all intact. This is when I started to find humor in my relationships with men- it was a joke! Being a proficient writer, I wrote many articles and short humorous stories that categorized obvious "relationship flaws" until a brick was flung full force at my skull!

When it comes to men, I'm a little slow! I always excused the obnoxious, selfish, irritating behavior because, like a wild little puppy, they were cute and fun to play with. This oversight led me to my newly perfected ritual of eliminating any trace of their existence… with the deleting assistance of liquid whiteout.

My organizer's address section has more whiteout than ink! There was pain… even though I'm glad I'm glossing over it. The stories I wrote were so obviously satirical and matter-of-fact, I spent endless hours laughing at my ridiculous choices! I was miserable but entertained. I did choose them, no one to blame but myself. I'm happy to report that although my sex life sucks (no more sexual flings), I've learned my lesson. If I don't want the same results, I need to change what I'm doing that always gets me what I end up being miserable with. And this little revelation only took me 10 years to get!

While I was exploring new ideas and tools regarding relationships, I somehow landed a part time job with a lady who put on regular lingerie shows.   I took it for the quick cash… I was still not at a point when my stamina lasted for hours, so I needed to make the most of them! She allowed me to wear the fun costumes that were already a part of my wardrobe (I had been dancing since I was young), and my bikinis that were just as sexy as the other girls without compromising my principles or feeling uncomfortable. I did intermingle some lingerie… under a cute leather jacket with thigh-high boots. I wore what I would feel OK with if my mother was there. I found I really enjoyed the drawing we did after each girl paraded her "outfit" around. She "sold" tickets to the onlookers for the big drawing to win a prize. After each romp around the restaurant, I would get on the microphone and announce the winner from the ticket I pulled.

Of course, being dramatic as I was, and always enjoying to make people laugh, I would draw out the time and tell jokes! I remember being told by the lady who hired me to keep it to a minimum – this wasn't "MY" comedy show! I didn't really hear her; I had my own agenda. That is how I formed "Monica's Laughs and Lace." I'm very entrepreneurial and I saw a way I could increase my profit, and best of all be the star of the show with my own business!

It took me about a month to make the break and take my show on the road. Although it was hard work, I did really well. My jokes turned into stories, mostly about my past and present disaster dates from Hell! Lucky for me (LOL) I still wasn't quite over my "sucky choices" phase. My life provided a LOT of material! I was very entertaining. My mannerisms and expressions when I spoke always cracked people up. I found a way to capitalize on that!

At first, I used humor to sidetrack the men. I didn't want anyone at my show thinking he could get turned on. I could sidetrack and sublimate their feelings by making them laugh! After a while, they accepted my "unspoken" terms! I loved being able to be as sexy as I wanted and still able to not only divert their attention, but to put women who were there at ease and not feel left out. Most of my routine was impromptu as I walked through the crowd with the microphone getting up close and personal, while bantering about some disdain over "penis envy!" I did have this and I wasn't ashamed to admit it! I proudly proclaimed if I had one, I probably wouldn't leave the house, as it was a plethora of pleasure! What the hell could be more fun?! They liked that! I felt powerful!

During that year, I performed at clubs under my stage name, Monica Michaels. I met some interesting people, hosted sports shows, modeled at trade shows representing my comedy spoof on the lingerie "models." A friend of Danny Bonaduce (from the 1970s TV show *The Partridge Family*) told him about me, and there was talk of me being interviewed on his radio show in Chicago – but I never followed that up.

I had to be available at any time to fill in, and I felt that was too much of a hassle to go through for an "iffy" chance! I guess I didn't really see what I was doing as any great feat – I found a way to pay the rent because of necessity! I wasn't able to work full time. Any enclosed environment with four walls, the same faces gossiping about whatever trivia of the moment was at hand, the cold glare of the fluorescent light that depressed the hell out of me was suffocating, stultifying, and unbearable! Basically, I was just doing what I always did… creatively construing some project to carry me until I moved on to my next endeavor. I enjoyed the release, it allowed me to vent about men and get paid to do it! I realized that I was working harder than I EVER did before for any boss… but it was MY creation, so I didn't mind so much.

When I wasn't working, I was reading, studying, and fervently absorbing everything I could get my hands on about death and relationships, including: *Surviving: When Someone You Love Was Murdered by Lula M. Redmond; Are You the One for Me by Barbara De Angelis; On Death and Dying by Elisabeth Kubler-Ross; Personal Power by Anthony Robbins; The Power of Intention by Wayne Dyer; You Can Heal Your Life by Louise Hay; Anatomy of an Illness by Norman Cousins; Men Are from Mars, Women Are from Venus by John Gray* …just to name a few.

I realized I filled my life with two dichotomies: my incessant need to under-stand the meaning of death, and my unyielding quest to figure out how to live in the here and now and cultivate a good life with healthy relationships. I would be quite popular at a cocktail party with the knowledge I had acquired! (LOL)

No matter how much effort I put into making positive changes, I was still stuck – something was missing! In counseling I uncovered real pain that stemmed from my non-relationship with my father. I refused to give it any more attention than I felt it deserved. It is funny how the issues that I chose to repress, like a bull-headed irritant, refused to die! I finally got the message: "I couldn't beat them so I joined 'em." I decided to acknowledge, accept, and integrate my anger toward my distant father so as not to continue on the same dead-end path with men… I'm still working on it!

Today, seven years later, I feel I'm ready and open to love again. At least this is what I tell myself! In between the seven years there were casual dates, sexual encounters, and a stint of a three-year, more off than on again relationship. I stayed connected in some way with him because of our only common bond of grief – which he refused to talk about. Both of our sisters died the same year with no closure for the family. He was also very close to his sister, more than his other siblings. We were the same two years apart in age, and similar feelings about the relationship I felt with Jill. Thinking back, I think this was the only time he ever talked about feelings.

The rest of the relationship would be filled with me trying to pry open his heart. It never worked, but I didn't figure that out for a long while! The only thing I paid attention to that mattered at the time was how he didn't fear my being a Survivor of a violent, highly publicized murder. He didn't act like it was contagious, something others acted like, and he didn't see me as damaged material due to my unfortunate circumstances! He was a Mexican-American who grew up in a violent environment. The gang problem was improving, but violence wasn't something foreign you only saw on television for him! He shared with me the hardships of growing up in the inner city. I was shocked to find out the lack of resources that were available for them that suburbanites took for granted!

I was very attracted to him in a lot of ways. It didn't last, but it did die a slow, and lingering death! I take full responsibility for paying no attention to the red flags that screamed "he isn't ready to open up and trust!" His actions that mirrored his sentiment were obvious to everyone except me. The way he didn't make time for us; on the list of priorities I didn't top out the list; except to have sex (which eventually became too infrequent to even please me anymore – I couldn't stay excited through my anger toward his nonchalant attitude). I had to get totally fed up and sexually frustrated before I walked! This was the first time I ended it in a huff. Of course, we repeated this destructive pattern several times before it actually ended. When we were together, I paid no real attention to how unwilling he was to be open, loving, and trusting. He trusted no woman-he himself told me this, and wouldn't allow himself to be made a fool of ever again. His past girlfriends always cheated. I could never figure out why, he was really hot! It must have been them.

I was so wrong! The reason I didn't cheat is because Leos' are loyal – we don't cheat, we leave! This substantiates the number of times I broke it off with him. But time would pass, and my memory would lapse – I wouldn't be so angry, so of course I always went back. It usually took a holiday, like Valentine's Day or Sweetest Day, which meant nothing to him, so he didn't go out of his way for me. Then came my birthday, he didn't even get me a card! That was usually the straw that broke the camel's back! Any reminder of dear ol' distant nonchalant dad would send me raging. He told me later, after I calmed down enough to be willing to talk to him, that he had a card for me – but I got him so mad he didn't give it to me! This pissed me off even more! I began to find his inability to take a risk weak and a real turn-off. Our final breakup came when this repeated itself, and although I was willing to be friends, I was convinced I wanted a different boyfriend. I didn't want to date him anymore.

I even opted to be alone, when I cancelled a New Year's Eve date, when I finally realized I was setting myself up for a fall. This was the exact opposite of my desire! I wanted to have a healthy, happy, loving, relationship with a guy who was romantic, gentle, able to express his feelings and needs, and willing to work through his own "stuff!"

I knew and accepted that it was time for a change. No matter the price I had to pay, I needed to have faith that I could meet someone more compatible. I eventually left, without the anger I nurtured over the three years of wrestling with him, with only a little sadness and great disappointment. I found out when I got rid of the anger, I could handle the sadness underneath, because I was now open to letting someone else in. When I released the sadness, I also released a sigh of relief! Things made sense to me and I felt OK, not abnormal for not choosing to be married with children, which I had no desire to be! I was being true to myself, empathic to others' needs and feelings and not feeling lonely or desperate because I didn't have a guy in my life (not even a physical relationship to tide me over). I was open to meeting someone new with no distractions in my way to stop me! I admired my inner strength to be willing to love again, even after all the tragic losses of loves. I welcomed who the next guy was to walk through the door.

Nothing changes overnight, and time can be a real pain in the ass to wait for, but the first step of acceptance is the hardest, and I've taken it! Every week I work on this with my grief counselor, my confidant, my support system, my friend... she is a lifesaver! It wasn't my idea to pick up where I left off in therapy on relationships. I was consumed with only doing my grief work to survive, and laughing off the hypocrisy of my social life! It was her generous offer to work with me at a VERY affordable rate! She kindly extended this to me as she said she was touched by my kindness, by how beautiful I was inside and out, and yet unable to have a relationship, and she saw deep down how I was so sad. She could read between the lines. Through her observant empathy she could feel my pain, even through my humorous gestures. I was running around keeping busy, felt great, looked great, attracted all the guys I wanted, and had a beautiful new condo that Mom helped me get. What the hell did I need with a man other than sex?! I didn't realize I closed this part of me off- she did and was determined to help me relocate it!

I still didn't get it. In my own mind I was cool, independent, sexy, and aloof. I emulated my idol and mentor, Cher, who I was often compared to – this made me feel great! A beautiful, talented, independent woman, who... OK, had lousy luck with men LOL! I could live with that as long as I could attract all the "boy-toys" I wanted. I even had a band called "Boy Toys"; I obviously chose the name for a reason. The sexy, younger drummer was mine! He didn't mind, he even wrote me a song, *"She's a Star."*

Yes, par for the course, it blew up in my face eventually... but the ride was still fun! I didn't trust older men, anyone over 30. I still struggle with that one, and now that I'm there myself it throws a curve into the mix. (LOL!)

My counselor was concerned that a nice, sweet, beautiful young girl was purposely creating her own agony by making poor relationship choices that inevitably would explode, like the previous "non-relationship" relationships. She didn't want to see me so unhappy with all the hardships that I had already endured. If it wasn't for her, I don't know if I would ever have had the courage to confront these demons. I lived with them for so long, I actually made a place for them in my mind! I love her for her compassion and I thank GOD that I have the type of personality that is charming and infectious so people genuinely want to help me.

I worked and continue to work on the buried demons that taunt me when it comes to men! So much of it has to do with my dad… he didn't really want children. My mom insisted that they adopt me, and then two years later my sister Jill. Even kids didn't give them a closer bond. They were married for 27 years of my mother screaming and my father cruelly punishing her with his cold-hearted "silent treatment!" They stayed married for the kids – go figure! When the divorce finally came, it was his easy out to divorce his daughters too!

Mom used to tell me that when we were kids, he would play with me and ignore Jill. I felt so bad and guilty about this; I grew up as a teenager who was determined to make him suffer for all he did. I grew to hate him with every cell in my body! I haven't spoken to him in seven years, since Jill's murder. He disowned me on the day we were "celebrating" Gram's birthday – she was 80! We were to meet at this restaurant about 40 minutes from my apartment. It was 95 degrees and I had no air conditioning in my car. I asked him to pick me up – he didn't! He had to get his girlfriend and her son, and Gram; there was no room in the car, or it was out of his way, or some other lame ass excuse he came up with! I wasn't thrilled about the whole situation, but Gram asked me to be there for her, so I went.

When I arrived, I was about 10 to 15 minutes late. Send in the firing squad! To him, I was always late, my head was always in the clouds, and I would probably never grow up. I was past my late 20s. What a jerk!

When I arrived at the table, hot, uncomfortable, and sweaty, I intended to make the best of it for Gram's sake (whom I loved dearly). I should have listened to my gut reaction and turned around and left, or better still made a polite excuse over the phone for my absence, but I stayed. His aloof attitude toward our family irritated me. He was acting as if his real family- Me, Mom, and Jill, never existed! As if this new girlfriend of the moment who sat next to him was all he ever had! That bastard even referred to her son as if he was his own – he treated him better than he treated me and Jill! I couldn't stand this charade. It was turning my stomach! I sat there quietly trying to contain my fury. Gram kept making irritating references of how damn paternal he was… yeah, let's elect him for "Father of the Year" award! The same man who disowned his own kids, who never wanted to be a father, and who hadn't sent us birthday cards for 10 f***ing years!

Gram attempted to gloss over my contempt. They were both very good at glossing and hiding. Let's play our favorite game of "Let's Pretend!" Their relationship was lousy, even though my grandmother excused his rude, cold way of ignoring her. This also made me mad! *I* was the one who filled the role of a loving child who cared deeply for her. It was me who gave a damn that she had food every week. Since she didn't drive, I took her every Saturday since I got my license! I turned it into our afternoon outing. It was my mother who taught me about dignity. I never let her think she depended on me, instead it was me who cherished our time, and I didn't even consider it anything other than our cool afternoons together. So what, if I waited for her to buy some food at the grocery store… in my mind, I was lucky to have such a cool relationship with my Gram. That is what I called her. That, and G.R., for Grandma Rose.

I loved her so much… I didn't see it coming… I must have left my etiquette restraint back at the apartment, because it became open season and I was out to hunt me a father! If he didn't act so cool and detached for presentation purposes, I might have made it through the meal. Then the final dagger – he hands me a "foreign object" with a stupid grin on his face! What the hell was this? A birthday card? Why NOW, after 10 years of absence?! What was he trying to prove?! I held my tongue long enough to read the inscription. How dare he include "her"- some new stranger!

Was it so damn difficult to relate to me without all of these stupid women who mean nothing to me?! It wasn't as if he was married… Jesus, he just broke off his long-term fling with the "psycho-bitch!" I probably got my shitty choice-making talent from him!

I realize now that what I did next on impulse was wrong- I tore up the card, fighting back the tears. I couldn't believe anyone would want to be with him – he was such a fake! Oh, yes, he was good-looking and women dug him for this, I guess. My attack sent a reaction through him I had never seen… words flew out of anger, back and forth, each of us eager to draw blood! Then it happened… the final blow that severed any thought of a relationship between us. I screamed, "I blame you for Jill's murder – she married him because of how poorly you treated her! Her blood is on your hands!"

I don't remember at what point he was going to hit me… but instead, he exited the restaurant in a huff. I sat, pleased that I finally got a reaction out of that cold-hearted bastard. Even if I knew I was wrong, I felt vindicated! I sat there and finished my brandy-ice dessert without even flinching! I could still hear his words as he glared a hurtful stare with fury in what I saw as distant eyes… "I never want to see or speak to you again, Maureen, as long as I live." My smart-ass reply of "Gee dad, I sure will miss the every 10-year birthday cards, and the once a year phone calls!" It was pretty ugly; come to think of it, I don't even remember the other customers who witnessed this whole scene. To me, it was as if I was alone and at peace. I didn't pay attention to anyone else, nor was I aware of any discomfort they might feel. Not at that moment. I waited a long time to get that off my chest.

Thinking back, I wish I didn't say that to him. I wish my Gram wouldn't have also chosen to sever our relationship – the bond that I thought could never be broken. I was wrong. "Grandparents don't disown you because you behave badly, Maureen," my mom tried to console me. "Yes, you were way out of line and even obnoxious, but no parent disowns a child!" I appreciate her telling me this, but I still feel guilty! Another terrible loss! This was five years ago. It still hurts. I guess it always will.

Chapter Five: Man Plans... God Laughs

I was in a constant, desperate search of ways, tools, and ideas to somehow reassemble my life after my sister was killed. It seemed an insurmountable mountain to climb, so a lot of the time I spent in recovery. I would take a few steps forward, then collapse from exhaustion and irritability of having to work so hard just to function! I thought I was damaged for life. I would struggle with my reason for existence and end up going back and forth in my mind over my belief system, and lack of belief system. To say I was angry was an understatement. I was livid!

Then one day, I was writing a poem that was titled "The Bond." It was about how strong of a bond I felt with Jill, even in death. This scared me that the closest person I felt a connection with was dead. I felt a strong pull from inside me to lie down next to her. As I wrote the poem, tears streamed down my face and stained the paper. It was at this moment that I made up my mind. To live in this pain, I would have to find a very strong and powerful reason for my existence! I knew I had no choice, as any other option would be unthinkable to do to my grieving mother, who could barely breathe! I decided I was going to make damn sure that Jill didn't die in vain! And if I had to go through what had now become my life: the constant pain, heart palpitations, fear of my own shadow, uncontrollable anger that even scared me, nightmares, therapists, medication, counselors, support groups, more losses than there is time or desire to name- not to mention the hell of the holidays, anniversaries, birthdays, and all those other unexpected and unwelcome triggers that came out of nowhere with enough force to send me catapulting back to where I started- if I had to go through this, I damn well was going to make a difference!

Although I always saw myself as deep (you can feel it when you read my poetry, or listen to my songs), I went beyond what would be expected of anyone in my age bracket at the time. Nothing in everyday life could hold my attention – especially the "frivolous" chatter of nonsense stuff that consumed most office conversations. In fact, this made my stomach churn! I refused to engage in these types of conversations.

Right or wrong, all I could think in my mind while "they" rambled on about some insignificant "problem" was- I can't relate to one word you are saying! All of this is nonsense to me. How can you talk of such trivia when I've just "survived" (I use the term loosely and with sarcasm) the nuclear reaction that has left my life in total shambles?! I don't give a damn about your insignificant crap! To say I wasn't the greatest company and very anti-social would be putting it mildly!

I was really angry, confused, and fed up with the lack of empathy I found in the world of what I referred to as "civilians" – people who didn't go through what we had experienced. I was sickened at the attitude of our society toward grief and loss. The lack of validation and lack of education regarding treating people (in desperate pain) with kindness and sensitivity infuriated me! I feel it's absurd to expect someone who can't even function without walking into walls, as they're so grief-stricken, to return to work accordingly and continue to put their "square hole in a square peg" for a paycheck that paid for stuff that no longer really matters in the big picture!

I studied other cultures and their treatment of the grief-stricken, their attitude towards death, and what cultural ceremonies they practiced which showed respect, validation, and support. I was relieved to find that in some cultures, when people grieved, they hurled their whole bodies on the ground and wailed a high-pitched cry of mourning that wasn't only accepted but expected. When I did this, my boyfriend, best friend, and mom thought I needed to be put in a hospital! I don't blame them, they didn't know any better, and I must have been a pretty scary sight at that time.

This was what led up to me becoming such an emphatic advocate on raising awareness and increasing empathy for Homicide Survivors. This even led me to address the Democratic Convention that was held in Chicago during 1997, in the hopes of reaching just one person! My original quest was to stop a callous movie crew from filming our story against our will and without our permission! I knew it was necessary to reach the general public in relaying the trauma and havoc the movie was creating for Mom and me!

I emphasized how we were no different from any of them, and although they may not relate today, there is no sanction providing a guarantee for the future. How would they feel in our shoes? People came up to me after I spoke and expressed a feeling of gratitude for articulating and standing up for people who had no voice. You would think this would make me feel good-it didn't! It clarified how uphill my struggle would continue to be. Looking at my mom, friend, and attorney from across the platform, I remember getting this nauseous feeling for how horrible it was for her to hear her surviving daughter speaking out for what was right against multi-billion-dollar movie conglomerates. The unsettling mixture of sorrow for the actuality of this day and pride in me for taking a public stance and wanting to make a difference- my heart went out to her!

After it was all over, I was left with the same question: who was I after Jill's murder, and what was it that I needed to do with my life to make a difference?! Even through my bouts of strength and courage, I still came back to the downfall of the aftermath that was unavoidable.

I had become more reclusive than ever, and after a public endeavor like this, I was bedridden for weeks. I still felt a closer bond to Jill in death than anyone in this world. I no longer considered even the thought of giving it all up, but the feeling of death still lived inside me! At first, I thought I was going crazy. I quickly countered this notion with all of the information that supported the sanity of my "crazy antics!"

OK, so I'm *not* crazy... I was still desperate to find answers to find an antidote for this excruciating pain. I sought out people who could identify, and I started to read everything I could get my hands on about loss and surviving after murder. I contacted and participated in many support groups: Compassionate Friends (an international grief group), Parents Of Murdered Children (POMC), Homicide Survivors, and Sibling Grief groups. I attended conferences and seminars and became certified after completion. Through one of my conferences, I ended up participating in a close-knit group for professionals in the field. The leader, who spoke all over the world, felt I was qualified and would be an asset to the group.

With death as my focus, my friends were the first to bring to my attention how much of death I resembled! My wardrobe of all black, with my now gothic look along with my "cheerful" disposition, was a little unsettling for some of them. I felt very comfortable! I knew they had a point, and I decided to integrate "bits and pieces" of life stuff. I added to my repertoire less nauseating subjects. However, I never did give up the black wardrobe- it is my calling card, and I wear it well! I naturally returned to what I knew. I started to talk about my relationships with men, which always led to a flippant comment or two that amused and entertained my listeners. LOL! I had a new-found love of comedy – especially doing a spoof on the actors I adored!

It was then that it all hit me. Here I was, six years of grief work later, and I'm really only back to where I originally started with my "stuff" before Jill was killed! This didn't make me happy! I didn't have a clue what to do now. How was I going to make up for all that lost time? This wasn't what I planned my life would be! Of course, I followed this thought of disgust with my usual pun; "Oh well, man plans… God laughs!" I got the picture. I didn't have the luxury of changing my reality, so I had better figure out how to play the hand I was dealt! Deep down, I wanted to learn to love and trust again- but what I wanted and what I actually believed would be attainable were two different stories!

In my mind I might as well ask for the Moon and the Stars while I'm at it. I was just about as likely to get them too! You probably see that I was a little lacking in the faith department. I not only didn't accept the notion of "ever after," the idea of putting "happily" in front of it made me gag! I made a friend of this sarcasm and though I wasn't thrilled with my reality, my highly developed sense of humor took the sting out!

Eventually, a very long time after this revelation, I began to see how I was actually feeling a little better and considered the possibility that I could be happy again. I stumbled onto something great, I thought to myself. Here I had spent years desperately searching for a key to get out of my pain, and there was no actual key to be found. I needed to make my OWN key! I needed to take parts of everything that I was learning and accumulating and put them all together to form my own individual key to a good life.

I can't stomach the cliché, "key to happiness"- it is just too… cliché! I discovered that it was the addition of laughter that completed the key. It seemed to smooth out the rough edges of the metal. It was humor that now opened doors for me. I want to clarify that none of those would be possible without all the hard work that led up to the integration of humor in my life. I needed a foundation to build on- humor allows me to build a stronger, more indestructible fortress!

Chapter Six: My Gratitude Journal was Empty

In the midst of my struggle to put some semblance of my life together, I came up with a hypothesis that was leading me to believe I could smile and even laugh and enjoy things again: there is a positive physiological effect that directly relates to the experience of an elated feeling due to the physical and chemical release, regardless of the depressed or despondent state the person is in! There was hope for me yet! My most insurmountable obstacle was my inability to continue and sustain any encouraging actions. With every step I took forward, I seemed to take three backwards, which cost me many years. That only added to my distress! I remember listening to Oprah talk about keeping a *"Gratitude Journal."* My first submission was, "I'm grateful that after all the hell I've been through, I can still be grateful for anything!" I laughed at the cliché that seemed not only fitting, but a good place to start! It worked… I was also grateful that something as wonderful of an escape as humor was available, and vastly becoming a well-recognized and respected "field of study!"

I found something new to focus my attention on. This made my horrific life almost… palatable! On the days I couldn't stand any noise or contact from the outside world, because I felt too "raw" to counter the clatter, humor was my only acceptable companion. Its presence was as warm and comforting as cuddling with a soft, furry puppy! I noted in my head all of the positive effects that followed what I now referred to as my "Time Out Humor Rituals!" I was destined to gather any information on humor to statistically and scientifically verify my hypothesis. I wasn't alone. I found experts in various fields who originally had the same quest. A forerunner in the field of Humor and its undeniable correlation with healing the body was Norman Cousins. He is well known for using the addition of humorous television comedies with his traditional medical model to combat hours of pain, in attempting to cure himself of a rare disease. His attempts were proven to be successful in alleviating a lot of the pain. This had the effect of allowing mind and body to be in a calmer state, where healing was a natural process that could be attained.

I believe in the mind, body, and spirit connection, and how the effect of one on the others can be achieved through a meditative process of calming the mind and body, so the natural ability to help ourselves heal can take place. You may be asking, "how does this relate to humor?" It is relatively self-explanatory.

Humor gives us a gift, whether we recognize it or not. It allows us to release tension and toxins that block our ability and/or desire to heal.

In this relaxed state of openness, even in a severely depressed person, this effect of brain chemicals is taking place on an involuntary basis. On a subconscious level, it is sending the message of "it's going to be OK, eventually." I use the word "eventually" for those of us more stubborn souls who refuse to allow too many good things in at once for fear they have no permanence in our lives.

The more I said it, "Humor Heals," the more I integrated the notion in my life. This set off a series of positive domino effects on all levels. The same areas that were negatively affected when my sister was first murdered, dare I say that now… thank GOD, could be rebuilt in a constructive manner with a stronger and more stable foundation. This doesn't by any means say that another loss wouldn't send me into a tailspin. Any loss now brings up all the crap that I went through, and there is no way to deny this reality. What I have today that I didn't have then are tools. Coping skills, the ability to ask for help, recognizing the necessity of support systems, newly developed cognitive awareness of how I've survived the worst already (this is very empowering), and the accumulation of the things I've garnered since I started on this journey.

My interest quickly turned into a passion that consumed me. I spent a great deal of time reading about others in this field who I could relate to. I wasn't too surprised to find, though many experts originally were pursuant in finding answers to a personal healing quest, there was no one who was a Survivor of a violent public death that was desperately grasping at anything to find some sense of peace! I felt that it was necessary as well as personally cathartic to tell my story. There was no one for Homicide Survivors to connect with, and this was a group of people who desperately needed to find support and compassion in the commonality of the trauma that now bound us together for life!

The one book I found most helpful, although the author herself wasn't a Survivor of a violent death, was *"Surviving: When Someone You Love Was Murdered."* There was a compassionate validation that Lula M. Redmond, the author, relayed that made griefwork and the fear of what lay ahead workable. I recommend this book highly to any Survivor of violent death, so that they can see that their strange emergence of feelings, thoughts, and actions that seem out of the norm to their usual, has become the *"new"* norm. If it wasn't for books like this, and a wonderful support network of compassionate people, I can honestly say I would still be at the point of my first chapter, "The Beginning of the End." If I wasn't validated, I would never have taken the chance to learn and connect with others… even to trust and love again.

Working in this capacity brought hope, and with hope brought the human urge to bring things in that felt good. I see humor as a "miracle drug." It has made the "ickiest" of the "icky" … palatable! LOL! This miracle drug is available to all, just for the asking. It can't be bottled as of yet, so the large conglomerate companies with their astronomical price tags can't have the monopoly on it! LOL! Humor is readily available and all around us as long as we are open to it, free of charge (for the most part). It connects every human being of every race, color, and creed. We all enjoy a good laugh! Although humor preference is subjective and what is funny to one may not be shared by all, what is shared by all is the exhilaration that the release of laughter evokes. Humor makes the discussion of difficult subjects easier to digest. It allows a person (especially in pain) to be open to hearing the reality of a situation and "accepting" the input. In my eyes, a successful humorist wears several hats at once. She or he is an entertainer, an educator, a healer, a compassionate advocate, a support system, and a "supplier of warm fuzzies!"

I'm so inspired by people who have struggled to overcome a great trauma, loss, or physical illness and have found the integration of humor to be their savior! I never tire of reading their biographies! Now humor therapy has become so expansive, even traditional steadfast institutions are studying and integrating the positive impact when educating physicians, nurses, hospice workers, grief interventionists, crisis counselors, and other such caregivers on the use of humor while working with patients. It is encouraging to see this transition take place, and I'm sure that over the next decade we will discover any inadvertent positive "side-effects!"

Chapter Seven: Acceptance of Reality… Grieving Does Not go Away!

I finally got it! The holidays kept coming, the reminders would always pop up out of nowhere, unannounced, with no warning time to get my bearings. This was part of surviving the loss of a loved one. The common terminology that is used to describe the "grieving process;" Healing, moving through stages, integration, surviving, and catharsis. The reference that churns my stomach is "getting on with your life!" They all seem to imply that there is an end – a place you get to where grief is somehow placed behind you. I realized why I fought this as many people in my position do, especially parents of murdered children, like my mom. Stripped of everything we once knew; we are now forced to reinvent a life without our loved one! A life without Jill?! Unheard of, and unacceptable! "I refuse!" It wasn't until I integrated my sister not being here, and this is *"key,"* in my life as I'm now reinventing it, that it allowed me to move forward. It seemed that the tools out there were focusing more on moving beyond, rather than moving *"with."* I realized that once I could bring Jill *"with"* me, I could go forward and build a life I love; I needed the validation to go forward *"with"* Jill.

Although our mannerisms, beliefs, and even actions may appear incongruent with what you, the outsiders, expect and desire for us… it isn't about what others expect, it is about how we are going to move forward to build a healthy lifestyle. There will always be the integration of our sadness over our loved ones not going forward in the physical realm with us. I've become aware of many things as a Survivor of Jill's violent death. As I type, my eyes fill with tears… I'm talking about my sister, the sister I was inseparable from… in my mind, my better, more stable half! I see her sitting next to me, the way she would quietly sit with calm acceptance I never felt from anyone else. I feel her; when she would hug me, she had such a vulnerable, close, open way of hugging me. I hear her; when she would say hello to me, she would say "sister" in an endearing, warm, loving way.

When all of this comes up for me, and the tears start to flow, I'm no longer a detached Survivor of violent death. I'm there again, not necessarily always at the scene of her murder, but the grief is in my body, and it cries out to be released! This was the lesson: Releasing my grief is *NOT* releasing my sister Jill!

She will always be my sister; I will always cry bittersweet tears when I think of her, and allow my senses to feel. I loved her more than I loved myself. Right or wrong, that is a fact! There's movement in the grief process, and as excruciating as the first years are, the rest of your life will also be a part of that processing.

There's no end to grief and sadness over loss when there is true love, and there was no end to that love.

So, many cynical people may say, "why bother if there's no relief in sight – if the grief never ends, what's the use of even working through all that pain?! Why not shut off feelings and put it behind you, just don't talk about it, like it never happened?" After all, if you never experienced the loss, then you couldn't be as grief-stricken and feel the wrenching in your heart. I'll tell you why I chose to do all the work to obtain the tool I realized (in the beginning, I didn't "accept") I would need in order to even get out of bed for the rest of my life! Because out of my only two choices, to reconnect or disconnect, I saw what disconnecting looked like from my own family members, and it was ugly! My mother and I were the only two of any of my family who chose to reconnect; I decided if I had to be here, and walk around with this heaviness inside my heart, I was damn well going to be here and make a difference!

My grieving will never end; I don't expect it to. With tools, support, compassion, therapy, and love, I can make a place for sadness so it will not try to consume me ever again. This was my most difficult and enraging lesson; I could no longer exist fighting against the wave. I couldn't deny my anger, sadness, and frustration. I couldn't deny myself from feeling the waves of the emotions I was so overwhelmed with when Jill was alive! That's who I am! I'm a very deep, emotional, compassionate, passionate female who loves and feels a gut-wrenching, at times immobilizing pain, which comes out in my poetry and my songs. To deny these feelings is to deny a large part of who I am.

I could have continued to learn this lesson through all the losses and unhealthy relationships I had with men! I didn't *NEED* my sister to be murdered! For this, I'll always be angry! When I hear someone look at my life and comment how I turned a trauma into a triumph, I want to puke! I'd give up everything to have Jill back! In this incidence, I wasn't given any choice in the matter – GOD didn't consult with me first!

Chapter Eight: There is A Light at the End of the Tunnel...and a Glimpse of it Somewhere in the Middle

When you're a Survivor, it's natural to feel so overwhelmed and disconnected to life that you want just to go inside to find a safe place to hide. My choosing to be reclusive and withdrawn from the world was how I coped when I could barely breathe from the intense pain. My grief encompassed my life! I didn't see far ahead and I knew my reality if I stayed stuck, wouldn't be one of my choosing but one of my making... I needed help! Sometimes when you're dealing with cumulative grief, different emotions get entangled... one of which is depression. This is something I've dealt with all my life, being diagnosed with Seasonal Affective Disorder, (SAD) as it is referred to, a few years prior to losing my sister in such a violent way. It became even more challenging now having trauma added to the mix!

SAD, which is a severe winter depression, consumed my energy every onset of winter. I would become what looked like a different person in the dark days of winter. I slept more than I was awake and I had to use Light Therapy every day just to get out of bed! My zest for life was replaced with apathetic disconnect! Mimicking Bipolar Disorder, I sought out support groups like Depression and Bipolar Support Alliance (DBSA) and National Alliance on Mental Illness (NAMI) to find a place I felt like people understood. I wasn't alone! I was desperate to find answers as to why I had such a radical transformation in the winter and to seek solutions and tools to manage my depression. I found out that it was a chemical imbalance, and Jill was the first person to accept me and to tell me how this wasn't a judgment of my character, it was a brain disorder; I felt heard and validated by her loving support.

Now as a trauma Survivor, I felt even more raw and exposed which drew me to run and hide from the world. I felt that life was asking too much of me... I was depressed, angry, and barely functioning because of how losing my sister intensified my emotional roller coaster! I lost my biggest support person, and I couldn't see how I was going to get through the next day, let alone my life without her! That's what the tunnel felt like... it was a deep, dark hole with no end in sight!

But in reaching out for help, joining support groups, reading everything I could get my hands on, listening to Progressive Thought Leaders like Wayne Dyer, Louise Hay, Tony Robbins, and Grief Specialists like Ken Moses, I came to the realization I Wasn't Alone! That was when the real shift came to not only accept what had happened, but to surrender to the myriad of feelings and learn to let them wash over me.

Everyone in the darkest place feels like they are the only one who feels the way they do. When we are shown that there are others who walk in similar shoes in life and that the pain is universal, we are able to accept our plight and surrender to the sadness. Knowing that this too shall pass, I'm going to be OK... I'm a *Survivor*! Through the tears emerges a stronger, more resilient person who would never have chosen this journey, but through tragedy I became who I'm in the world today. I would trade it all to bring Jill and Mom back, but I don't get that option. I have to choose how I'm going to play the hand dealt me. I remember the day I decided if I'm going to be here in the world without my family, I'm going to be here for a reason! Through the years of turning to my songwriting with my keyboard, my story unfolded in my music through the tears, the fears, the anger, the confusion, the strength, the faith, the conviction, and the belief!

One day, I just awoke and made the choice to live with conviction and accept the cards that were dealt me by turning the *Pain Into Purpose*! I couldn't go back to who I was; I needed to reinvent myself and my life in order to want to be here in the world. This was no small undertaking and would evolve into my life's mission, though at the time, I was merely grasping for a life jacket to keep from drowning! I knew how to ask for help and to get the support system I needed, as well as delving into researching everything I could find on how people survived trauma and coped with cumulative grief.

I wanted to regain my passion that I lost when Jill was killed! I grasped for anything I could hold onto that would give me a glimmer of hope. My determination to find a purpose for being in the world led me to seek out many avenues. Luckily, as I attempted this endeavor, more of the "me" I remembered started to emerge. My *savior* was a humorous approach to things.

My quick-witted style of communication also helped to pave the way. It opened doors and garnered the help I needed to attain the necessary tools to release the feeling of being victimized and choosing to be a *Survivor*!

The pain didn't subside, but my purpose exceeded the grief long enough to transform my attitude and give me the perseverance I needed to make this shift. It was the most challenging thing I've ever done… finding reasons to want to live now without my best friend, my confidant, my biggest support system... my sister. With tears rolling down my cheeks, I stepped into my new life. I surrounded myself with people who were empathic and compassionate. I researched every healing modality I could find to lessen the pain to help me focus on my purpose. The more Grief Work training I acquired, as well as the balancing of the intensity with Humor Therapy I studied, allowed me to be able to feel the release of the intensity of the grip of grief around my heart.

Building a Humor Library that consisted of things that made me laugh and using it on a daily basis allowed me the ability to do the necessary intense Grief Work. Laughing, even when it's choreographed, as I previously mentioned, releases the healing endorphins, which counters the pain and depression that's evident when you're a *Survivor*. This daily routine allowed me the ability to be more open-minded to finding a life I could love again. Laughter helped me to reconnect with the "me" I lost, and became the catalyst to my not only surviving, but eventually, thriving!

So, you see how the progression of healing works: First, your grief must be validated and supported, next, you need to acquire a new set of skills to live as a *Survivor,* bring in humor to release the constriction of grief, and research everything you can find on healing and surviving after trauma. I leaned heavily on my music to purge my emotions, as well as journaling and writing songs and poetry. Once I was on this Healing Path, I started to feel more comfortable in my skin. I chose to call it my *Healing Journey*, as that's what it feels like to me...a journey in pursuit of healing. I ended up putting out a CD titled *"Healing Journey,"* that also tells my story of trials and triumphs as a *Survivor* through my intense lyrical fusion and melodic entrancement designed for the listener to feel the flood of healing through their body. I found my light after I spent a long time in the tunnel of my grief. It doesn't come overnight, but with a willingness to want to find your way and a desire to live again after the trauma, with the acceptance of being a *Survivor* we can again find that light!

Chapter Nine: Not Another Stage of Grief! Does it Ever End?!

The last thing I want to do is write! My mom told me that is exactly why I need to. I need to show what the pain of reorganization looks like for others in their own grief process. It looks ugly! It's a dark, lonely, cold, empty vastness that feels timeless… as if I will never feel like myself (as I remember) again. I've lost my confidence – I feel like a stranger in my own body. I look around my room at clothes that I used to parade around in, in a comfortable and confident manner… and they seem like they belong to another person. I can't seem to put on my own jewelry… it's like I'm trying to disappear. I'm having a difficult time taking care of myself, and I can't stand my reflection in the mirror! I'm so sad…

I was flying in the summer. I had faith, hope, a dream… I was working so hard on getting my life together. I've been working with my counselor and friend on childhood issues that were holding me back. I was moving beyond my own grief work to stuff before Jill's murder. She helped me to see how I was stuck at a stage where I stagnated, and never had the energy and time after Jill was murdered to focus on old issues until now. How the hell can this be what sent me spinning out of control?! All I wanted to do was do whatever it took, in order to have a life with healthy relationships!

Yet, here I sit, curled up in a ball… afraid to speak, scared of my own shadow! No one who knows me would recognize me hiding and reclusive. I found myself asking friends and family to tell me about the Maureen Joy they knew… I so longed to be her! I felt like a fraud! I'm afraid to go out into the world to connect with a loving mate, to make the mark I always believed was my destiny… now I just don't see much value in a life of existence. But it is the best I can hope for at this time. I hate this place! I hate everything! I'm such a failure! I can't do anything right! I feel like I can barely keep up with everything and everyone! My life is taking a toll on me and it was only a matter of time until I snapped!

The straw that broke the camel's back was the decision to begin interior designing my dream condo. This meant replacing the brown wood furniture pieces with contemporary black lacquer.

As I always do when I'm reorganizing, I called Salvation Army to pick up the perfectly good, yet wrong color scheme furniture. I was in such a frenzy, I excitedly gave away the four bags of clothes, Jill's shoes (two sizes too big for me), two suitcases also filled with clothes, lamps, and end tables. I just kept getting rid of things that I felt were no longer fitting for me. I kept thinking of these things as clutter, and I was determined to reorganize every aspect of my life inside and out!

At the time I was taking this step, I remember feeling secure and pleased with my initiative. Having it in my life no longer fits – give it to someone who will use and enjoy it. It seemed fitting to also give away the brown wood bookcases and Jill's shelves to my friend who unexpectedly stopped by and just happened to be driving his truck. I thought, "two birds with one stone." I wasn't really thinking about what I was actually doing, and how I had those damn shelves for the past eight years! I wasn't prepared for the repercussions that I would inevitably be faced with. I happily (it was a warm, sunny day) hauled the bookcases to his truck with him. The next stop was Mom's; we brought over the recliner I had that was also Jill's, in order to make room for the black leather couch I was getting for my birthday present from a good friend. My mom also got caught up in the "let's give it all away" frenzy… she ended up giving my friend a 27" TV, offered him dishes, lamps, whatever he needed for his new apartment. Both Mom and I were feeling "let's get rid of everything!"

It didn't hit me until I walked back into my apartment, now that I had this open space. It felt strange and unfamiliar. I didn't feel comfortable. All I could see was a scary place! This wasn't what I had in mind when I thought about inventing my "dream condo!" I looked around the room… all I could see was the awkward space and furniture that no longer looked right. Nothing seemed to fit anymore! I intellectualized that I was just in shock. It will pass, and tomorrow I will wake up refreshed and excited about what I was doing – recreating a new life with a home that is filled with my personal touches, furniture, and accessories that reflect my personality.

I wasn't prepared for what lay ahead and the intensity of my emotional turmoil. I woke up in the middle of the night – my heart was racing, the same palpitations I felt when I knew a relationship with my past boyfriend was ending. I was hysterical. I was crying and frightened of what I had done in haste! I was shaking at this loss. I finally got it; it was another loss! I gave away furniture that belonged to Jill! As far as I was concerned, I had no emotional attachment, so this outburst of hysteria caught me totally off guard! In a fit of anxiety, I called my friend and woke him up in the middle of the night, begging for his understanding – he did. He told me he would just bring the furniture back until it was comfortable for me to part with it. This gave me the relief I needed in order to get through this. He gave me the option to leave it with him, or to have him bring it back. With this security net, I felt strong enough to try to live without the furniture and stick to my original plan of reorganizing.

The first week I was in pain. I felt awkward, scared, and exposed, but I still chose to try another week without it. The second week was just as bad, but I was aware of exactly what I had done, and my counselor validated my reaction and feelings of loss… I persevered. The third week wasn't much better, but I now had my new couch and I was trying to accept that everything new feels awkward – even things that we love. The fourth week I started to try to sit in the open space without hiding. It became apparent that I had built a fortress to surround myself with tangibles that I felt filled the empty space inside. This was a hard realization and one that I resisted all the way to getting healthy. This was seven months ago… in August 1999. Now it is March 2000… Had I not rewritten this chapter to put in the computer, I wouldn't have recalled how miserable I was.

I look around that same room today, and I see the beginning of a dream condo that is a reflection of my creativity and style. It still doesn't have the finishing touches, but I've found a way to position the couch that overlooks the beautiful skyline. The lighting is balanced and warm, and I'm starting to visualize how I will design my living room. If I didn't live through all I did, I would have had a hard time relating to the intensity of emotions that are even more prevalent in my life now, after Jill's murder.

I've accepted that triggers will keep coming, unannounced, and catching me at a time that is always less than convenient. The one thing I can count on is that it doesn't end. As long as I'm alive, I will experience another stage of grief. As long as I will love my sister, I will grieve her murder. My hope is to be able to ask for the support I need at those "trigger" moments and to continue to cry, laugh, and love.

Chapter Ten: I Practice what I Preach

When I set out to write this book, I solely did this as a cathartic release, in order to find some order in the chaos of emotions inside me. I figured if I kept writing, the feelings would find a home, and I could go out into the world again with an inner strength (an inner strength that was shredded when Jill was murdered). I was very clear about how devastated and shattered I felt inside, but I refused to let that be my fate! I've always loved to laugh… now I laugh to live! I couldn't believe how powerful and healing laughter is. With consciously integrating this into my life on a daily basis (like medications), I could put a toe back into the ocean of life, and perhaps even… swim.

I went from reading everything I could get my hands on that related to humor and healing, to studying the physiological and psychological benefits of humor, to researching the practical and professional humor skills that are effective learning aids in business. My heart brought me to do something that I felt made a difference, and in conjunction could also support myself. I didn't know where to turn, other than to open my heart and follow that path. I'm proof that humor heals even the most shattered of souls. Through surrounding myself with humor skills and tools, I'm also able to feel sadness without clouding it with other emotions.

I sit here and tears run down my face… I want to share my life journey with Jill. I want to call her on the phone and tell her how great it felt after years of developing my program *"Corporate Comedy Capers"* to stand up and deliver it successfully to businesses. I wanted to hear her say she was proud of me and she always knew I would make it! I wanted her to come over and sit with me on my balcony. I wanted her to take in the beauty of the Chicago skyline with a relaxing glass of wine as she quizzed me about astronomy, believing that I would now be able to connect the stars for the Big and Little Dippers (I still need her for this!).

I hear all the grief specialists, spiritualists, and believers. I know she's in my heart forever. But I want her in my life dammit! I want to hang out with her, tell her about the guy I'm dating, and be taken for a ride on her motorcycle!

It is this adamant attitude of rage (although under control now) that would have been my destruction if I hadn't done the necessary grief work, which included and always will include personal growth and a lot of humor. There's no way I could have gone to the depths of my soul and wander in the darkness of the hollow pit if I hadn't had the release of humor. I'm very clear there is nothing funny about trauma and tragedy – it flat out sucks! The stages of grief are not an option.

If you're a thinking, feeling, human being with a heart, you will travel this road. I decided that instead of doing what I had always done, which got me the opposite of what my objective was, I would surrender to the pain! The physical agony, the emotional upheaval, the medications, the therapy, and the support groups- anything and everything necessary in order for me to go on living!

I feel this is very important to differentiate between the too casually vocalized statement of others (who don't know any better) "to go on living" versus "to get on with your life." It may sound like menial semantics, but I'm a firm believer in the power of words, and how cathartic it feels for those of us who can't even fathom a life without our loved ones, to hear a validating statement that supports our grief process - no matter the timetable, as it is different for everyone. I feel it's so important to raise the awareness of the necessity for others to accept that we are not, and never will be, the same as we were before our trauma. This doesn't mean we will be victimized the rest of our lives, nor does it mean we will remain immobilized by our grief on an ongoing basis. It DOES mean that we WILL change – we HAVE to in order to be able to function. Everything we knew is now gone.

We will have to reinvent who we are… this process takes time. Sadly, not everyone who was once close to me is in my life today. It's a horrible existence. It takes a person who has his or her own inner strength to be supportive. I realize people can only give what they have inside of themselves, but it still hurts.

The reality of my own life makes me shudder! I'm overwhelmed at what I have on my plate. Without the belief system that I'm here for a reason, I would have given up a long time ago.

But I get up every day and try again, because I have a purpose – to share with the world how important laughter is, and how it can be a valuable aspect in grief work. I figured in the worst-case scenario, I will continue to share this with everyone I meet in life and maybe touch someone who's in pain. Even if I don't become a famous Humor Therapy Guru, as I see myself in my own mind, (LOL) I've learned to laugh at myself. The difference is that I do it with compassion and integrity.

I had to let go of my incessant desire to control the universe. I get this from my mother, who even today is the queen of control. We both realize on an intellectual level how preposterous this need is. However, we still challenge this with every cell in our bodies! If you dare to combine this "attitude" with unbearable pain… let's just say it's less than pleasant to be around us when the pain collides! Luckily, we both look for humor in everything we do – and with our lives… there is always an abundance of crap to parody!

Ten years later…

So here I am, 10 years later. Mom lost the battle and died in my arms June 14, 2010- one week before her 75th birthday. Another loss… once again, here comes the grief! Ugh! Not only did I lose my mom, I lost my only connection to the trauma of Jill's murder and the shrapnel it left behind in the ruins! Who was going to be a witness to our devastation?! Mom and I grew bonded through this tragedy, and we were basically enmeshed, which is not always a good thing to be. But we were desperate to reconnect, and clinging to each other seemed to help us for a very long time… until it didn't.

Still in therapy, I grew healthier and learned to create healthy boundaries with everyone to have better relationships. I still struggled to move forward. Mom told me before she passed, when she knew she was dying, that I was going to be OK, no matter how much I protested through streaming tears not to leave me alone in this world. She took my hand, looked deeply into my eyes, and calmly proceeded to tell me how I will survive. Exactly how I will grieve but eventually be a strong and powerful woman who will make an impact on the world.

She told me I have to share my book and my music of empowering messages people need to hear. I, of course, was too busy protesting her saying goodbye to really listen. Looking back, I guess a seed was planted and when it was time, it bloomed and the flower's name is *Healing Journey*!

As I'm writing this, tears well up in my eyes. Yes, I've done and continue to do what I refer to as grief work to find my place in this world on my own. Along the way, I've lost many loved ones since my sister, my mom, my aunt, my closest friends within weeks of each other, and recently two more friends within the past year. I keep telling God, "Hey, I've had my fair share of loss… let me catch my breath already!" HE has his own agenda…

Grief is not linear, and there will be triggers along the way. Birthdays, anniversaries, holidays, just to name a few. The triggers can bring up sadness and a myriad of other emotions. But, when you reach out for support and you acquire healing tools that help you to navigate the rough patches in the road, the intensity of the grip of grief lessens, and eventually you do regain your footing. *"This too shall pass"* … words I would say aloud to myself with tears flowing like a river washing over me. I continue to get support while I'm out in the world reaching out to other Survivors who walk with pain.

Now we live in a tech savvy world, which allows us to reach people we never could before. A friend in the music business created my music page to share my music, and other empowering tools to navigate life, and living in recovery information. I can feel the shift as I'm finding my way back in the world in a healthy, loving manner.

I continue to pursue the quest to improve my life, help others in pain, open my heart, and share my *Healing Journey*.

The end… for now

CONTACT INFORMATION:

AMAZON.COM: I HAD TO LAUGH TO LIVE…

Book and Kindle

CD BABY: STORE.CDBABY.COM/CD/MAUREENJOY

EMAIL: MOEJOY2003@YAHOO.COM

FACEBOOK: MAUREEN JOY HEALING JOURNEY

WEBSITE: WWW.MAUREENJOY.COM

****

Amazon Reviews

Paula J. Battaglio

5.0 out of 5 stars **A Warm Hug of Authenticity and Humor**

May 10, 2019

Format: Paperback Verified Purchase

I loved this book! Maureen writes from a place of deep authenticity and honesty about her journey, which makes me breathe a deep sigh of relief about my own process. In reading about her experiences, I feel like I have a big sister who is wise, loving, and very salty who absolutely has my back. In this world of whitewashed political correctness, she is a breath of fresh air - someone with the courage to express how she feels, even if that truth is skewing a sacred cow or two!! I hear she has a CD as well, and will be offering her work in seminars and personal sessions. Take note - you will be hearing more about Maureen Joy very soon! It feels like her star is on the rise, and her warm, truthful and wise message will be reaching millions very soon. If you feel like your grief is unresolved, READ THIS BOOK!

****

Marti H

5.0 out of 5 stars **Funny and Heartwarming - Loved this Little Book!!!**

March 12, 2019

Format: Paperback Verified Purchase

This book is inspirational and an easy read. The author is funny and a real survivor! She understands great loss and offers insightful antidotes on getting through life's most difficult times. I highly recommend this book!!!

****

LINDA S

5.0 out of 5 stars **Very Touching and Helpful.**

April 25, 2019

Format: Paperback Verified Purchase

I met Maureen Joy 5 yrs ago. Throughout the years I've watched her "Walk her Talk". While reading this book (which is easy to read, specially with ADD) I laughed and cried.
Then I realized this isn't just any story, it's real...her life story!! She gives you tools to cope with all that your you're going through...most of all she gives you hope!!
So proud of you Maureen. Linda S

****

Lisa Golbeck

5.0 out of 5 stars **Everyone Needs Help on Their Healing Journey** ♥□

October 20, 2019

Format: Paperback

Maureen writes openly about her personal tragedy, and it is Inspiration! This is an interesting and helpful Story.
I recommend this read to help Everyone on their Healing Journey ♥□

Made in the USA
Coppell, TX
08 December 2021

67615103R00032